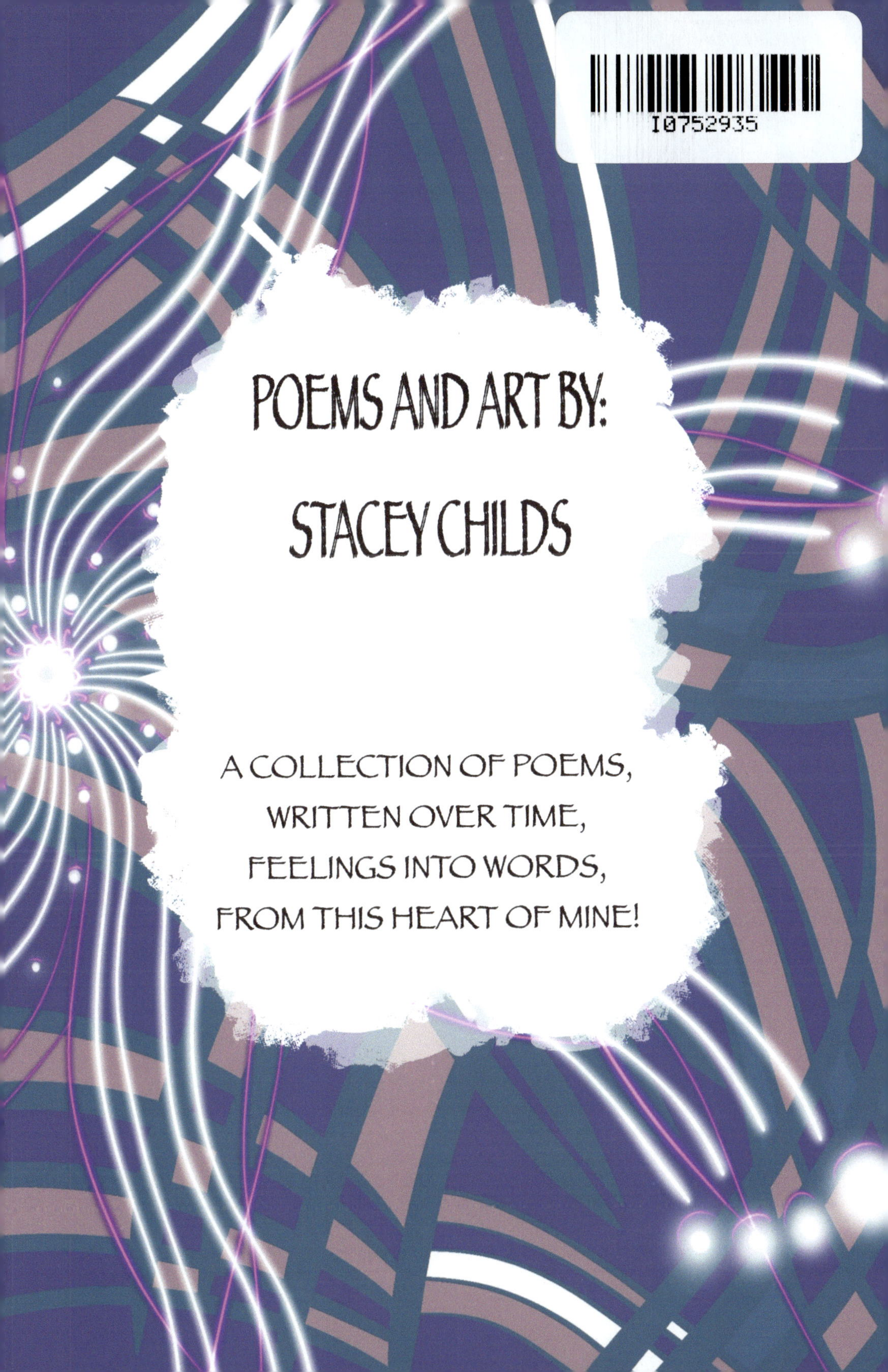
I0752935
POEMS AND ART BY:
STACEY CHILDS
A COLLECTION OF POEMS,
WRITTEN OVER TIME,
FEELINGS INTO WORDS,
FROM THIS HEART OF MINE!

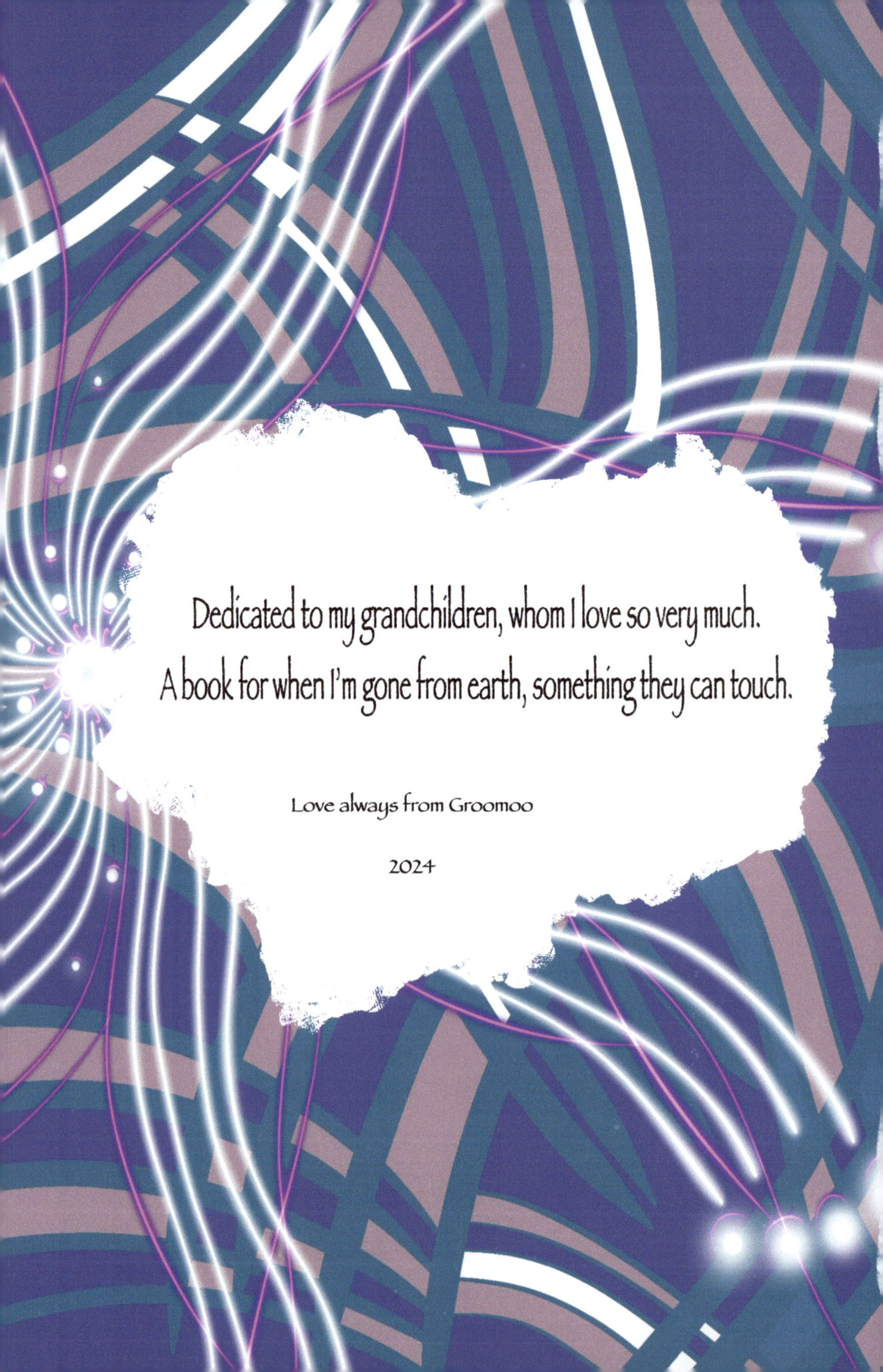
Dedicated to my grandchildren, whom I love so very much.
A book for when I'm gone from earth, something they can touch.
Love always from Groomoo
2024

ART LIFE

Imaginings and creativity,
means a lot to me,
making pictures for you and I to view,
makes me feel happy.

A thought arises in my head,
a picture then follows latter,
my hand gets to work with my pen,
turning my imaginings into matter.

Art is not for everyone,
for that I understand,
but for those of you who like a drawing,
I will share across the land.

For me art is life and it brings joy,
thought provoking or a laugh,
a moment of pause to have a look,
kinda like looking at a photograph.

My imaginings come, from in my brain,
but I pull them from the ether,
that beautiful unlimited invisible space,
where we can go when we need a breather.

Life is wonderful and exciting,
to see what happens next,
there are good and bad bits all the time,
that's the journey, to balance best.

So next time when your feeling down,
remember it will not last,
enjoy the good bits with the bad,
because life really does move so fast.

ONE LIFE

We have but one life to live,
moment to moment, breathe to breathe,
daylight beams and moon shadows,
time ticks, heart beats and love to give.

Happy days where smiles are stretched to their limits,
sad days where the covers stay pulled up,
those belly laughs times with good friends,
heart shattering shocks that make us want to go back a minute.

Sight for sore eyes, missed loved ones company,
bare feet in the sand and wind through the trees,
butterfly whispers and a magpie song, thunder rolls,
the smell of rain on dirt, more of this please.

The peaceful strum of an acoustic guitar, softly blown flute,
or the beat of the drum with some electric rock,
the sound of your furry friend saying hello,
what ever animal they may be, melted heart mood.

Soft things under your fingertips, a velvet or fluffy rug,
a warm fire on a chilly night, someone close to hug you tight,
a roof above to shelter the storm and sun,
grateful , thankful, competing with no one I wont say
.... I won.

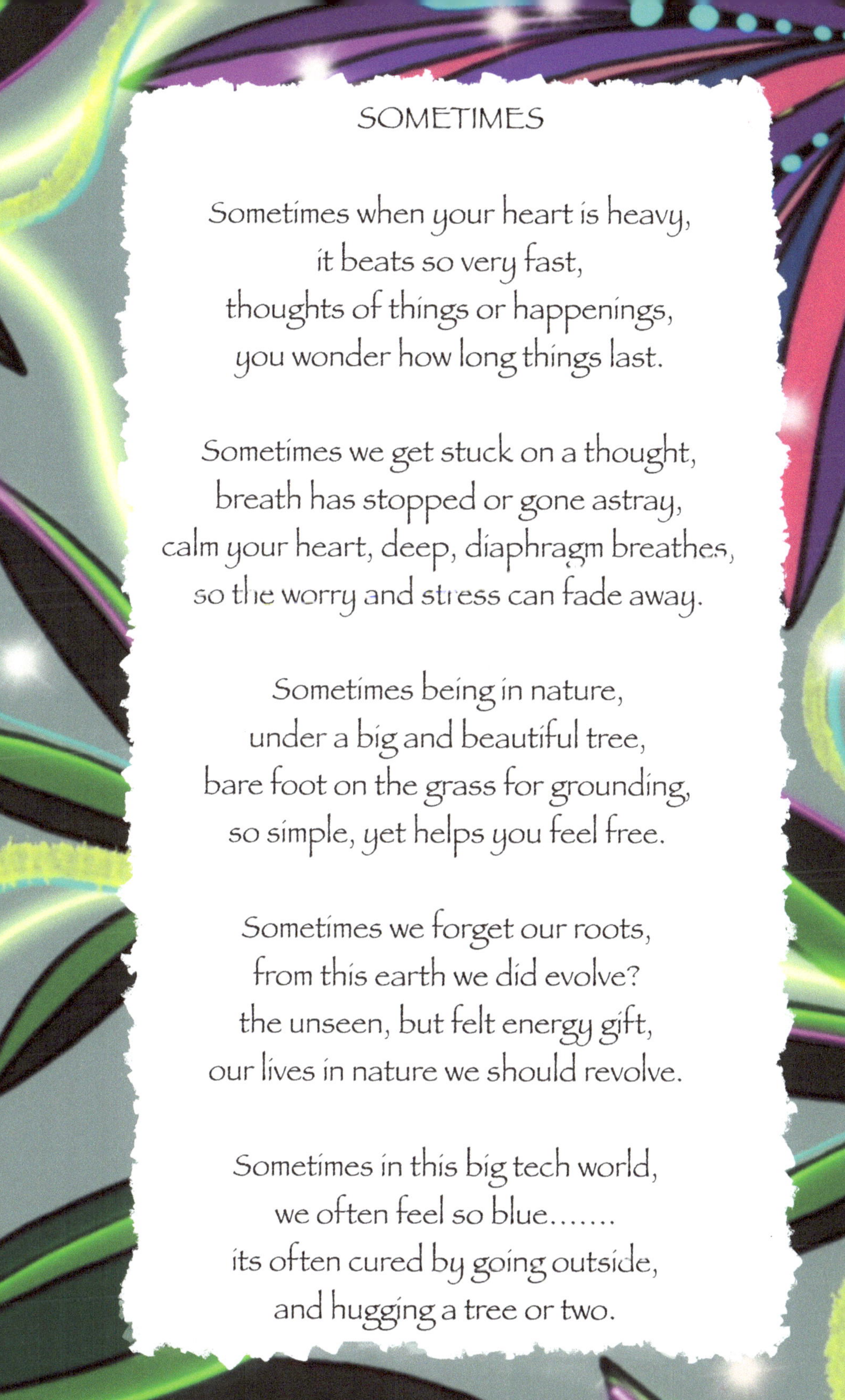

SOMETIMES

Sometimes when your heart is heavy,
it beats so very fast,
thoughts of things or happenings,
you wonder how long things last.

Sometimes we get stuck on a thought,
breath has stopped or gone astray,
calm your heart, deep, diaphragm breathes,
so the worry and stress can fade away.

Sometimes being in nature,
under a big and beautiful tree,
bare foot on the grass for grounding,
so simple, yet helps you feel free.

Sometimes we forget our roots,
from this earth we did evolve?
the unseen, but felt energy gift,
our lives in nature we should revolve.

Sometimes in this big tech world,
we often feel so blue.......
its often cured by going outside,
and hugging a tree or two.

SHADOW

There I am, there's my shadow,
moving with me throughout my life,
always, even when I'm happy or sad,
even if I’m in strife.

My shadow doesn't show my mood,
there upon on my face,
yet it’s right by my side,
through this life long race.

My shadow may be dark,
but that's just how it be,
without the beautiful light,
for it, you would not see.

Sometimes it is hiding,
when the world gets dark,
but when the sun shines bright,
it comes out, to make its mark.

We all have shadow,
a dark grey outline,
unlike a mirror,
with detail so fine.

A reflection for today,
for the darkness that’s in sight,
it could not simply exist,
without the presence of light!

Today I acknowledge my shadow,
it’s sometimes funny to see,
my way out of proportion,
exaggerated other me!

LIFE IS A JOURNEY

Life is a journey,
we all have to tread,
some of our steps are bouncy,
and some are filled with dread.

Our journeys are not the same,
each of us is unique,
our timelines, oh how they differ,
old and young, time passes,
It's just love we all seek.

Our journeys can seem mundane,
each day rolling into one,
but don't move so fast, stop,
breathe, slow down and feel the sun.

We must hold the vision,
life is a journey for us to create,
our dreams, desires and loves,
don't let them deflate.

The journey of life,
just do what you can,
learn to love who you are,
woman, teen, child or man.

Life is a journey, yours is your own,
be kind, honest and humble,
look for the good around,
no time to moan and mumble.

With life there are no instructions,
peaceful it is just to be,
to love and be love,
live in the now and be free.

SMILING BRIGHT

Smiling bright in the morning glow,
peace in the moment,
hearts full of wonder, flowers grow.

Water, earth, rainbows and vines,
life is amazing full of all sorts of times.

The mystic, the curious, the ever beating vibe,
looking at surrounds like for the first time.

I burst with joy with wind through my hair,
taking it all in, the whispers in the air.

I feel it, I dream it, for life is a lust,
just being present in the moment,
deep breathes is a must.

Smiling bright, for today is a gem,
caring is sharing a gift amongst men.

ONE DAY

Today the little things I am grateful for,
waking up, taking a breath,
step out of bed,
put my feet on the floor.

It's chilly today,
quite super cold,
this autumn morning,
I am another day old.

I drive to work feeling the sun on my face,
thank you Mother Earth,
for your warm sunshine embrace.

With a deep inhale, I look to the sky...
slow exhale no hurry in life...
don't worry about the how,
just work on the why.

The why do I do, what I do?
and where does my attention go?
this body will stop one day,
so just go with the flow.

Being in the now,
my immediate surroundings,
when I focus on my breath,
all around, are wondrous things!

No time for angry,
although I know there will be a time...
learn to master calmness,
for my heart to feel fine.

As the world rushes by,
by the clock by the measure,
I look within me, to find all the treasure.

I so cherish it all, as it will all end one day,
grateful for life in this body of mine,
The good, the bad so I'll play along the way.

WIRED

Wired houses, wired streets,
noisy city, rapid heartbeats.

Wired traffic lights, wired skyscraper,
so many buildings crammed into an acre.

Concrete boxes and wired towers,
designated areas only for the flowers.

Intersection traffic comes to halt
people scurry like ants,
orchestrated hustle style, by default.

Wired phones in offices, wireless outside surrounds,
frequencies of every sort, beam throughout the crowds.

Wired bodies, pods in ears, all eyes stuck in a phone,
people look the same almost like a clone.

Wired without cords, hooked on a system,
the matrix is real, just look at this prison.

Nature calls, trees speak,
time to get grounded 'NOW'
before the end of the week!

WORLD SEEMS DARK

Sometimes when our world seems dark,
and you cannot see your way,
sometimes just a little light,
can see you on your way!

Sometimes the dark can seem so much,
It's hard to find a way,
but all you need is a small spark of light,
to brighten up your day.

The dark can be, a glum old mood,
things happening you don't like,
all it takes is to smile a bit,
and you will start to feel alright.

Sometimes dark can pull you down,
where there seems no help in sight,
don't loose hope, the light will come,
just hold love in your heart so tight.

Think of the things that make you happy,
the things you have right now,
things that bring you joy,
like grass is to a cow.

If your feeling glum you see,
please know, you're not alone,
there is always someone out there,
just have a look in your phone.

Dial the number and have a chat,
if someone's on your mind,
I'm sure they'd love to hear from you,
being thought of is really kind.

Your feelings are valid, what ever they be,
wearing a smile or wearing a frown,
choose your vibration frequency,
high is mostly happy and low is mostly down.

I hope today your smiling,
and that you have found your light,
a little light in darkness,
in your heart, and in the night.

BEGIN AGAIN

As here in this room I sit,
thoughts, and ponderings,
thinking of a fresh start,
or a time to quit?.........

Not long ago, my heart was broke,
I've had some time to heal,
inner gazing, a time to rest,
and emotions that got woke.

Growth comes from pain,
as unfortunate as that is......
I just have to enjoy all of life,
it goes so fast... zip in a whiz!

The decision comes and goes,
do I give up on a goal, because it seems so far away,
or do I push on throughout the downs,
until its manifests one day?

Sometimes I think, all I needed was a rest,
time to reevaluate my direction,
let my heart heal to its best.

Creative feels are a funny thing,
the urge is not always there,
I find for myself that when worry is alive,
it goes away and that seems fair...

I like to draw mostly fun, happy things,
and dont like my sad ole art,
I like to put smiles on faces,
not sad things in your heart.

So with all that said,
I am back again, for a fresh new start,
I hope in time Ill just ride things out,
and always create my art !

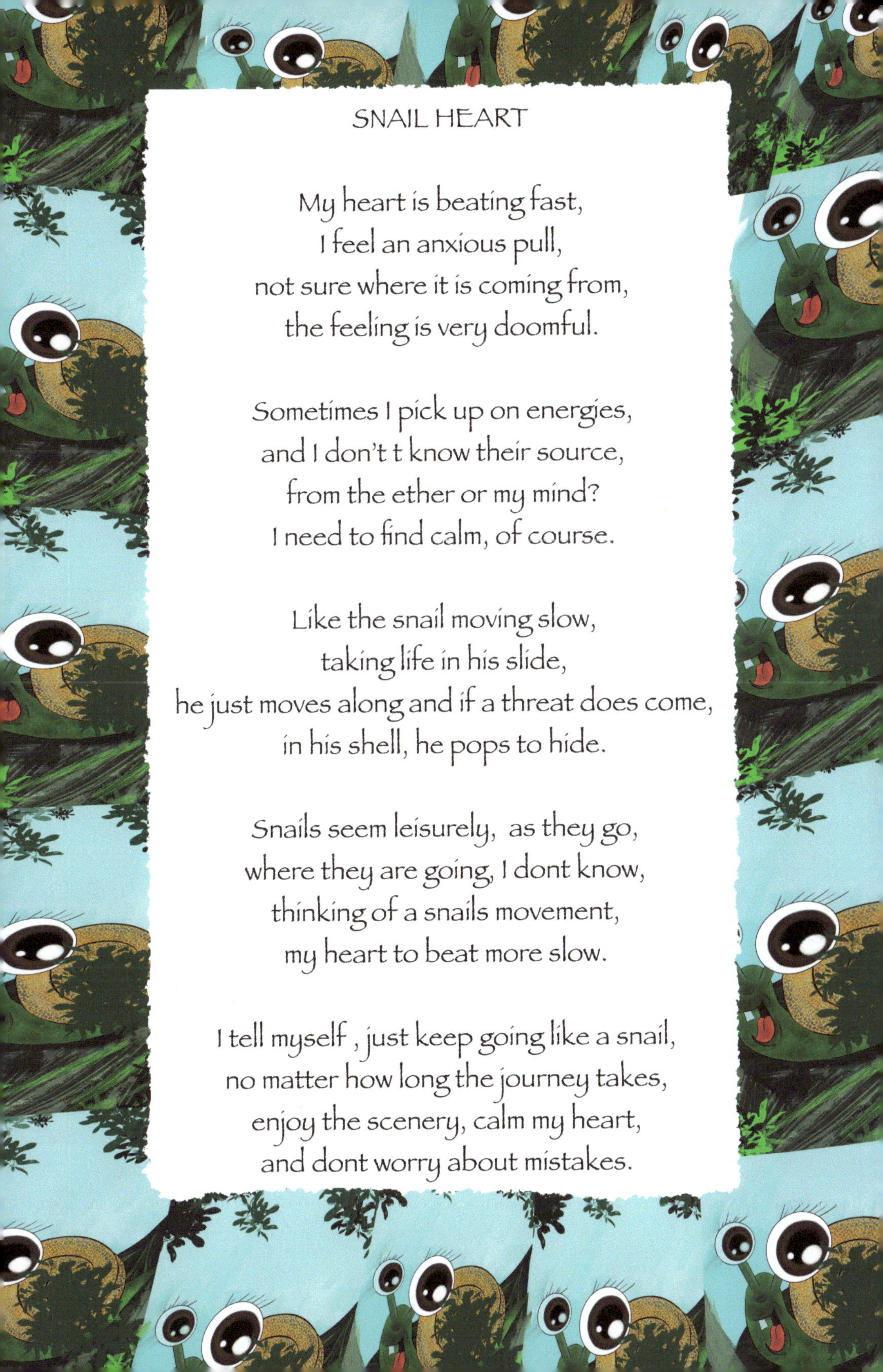

SNAIL HEART

My heart is beating fast,
I feel an anxious pull,
not sure where it is coming from,
the feeling is very doomful.

Sometimes I pick up on energies,
and I don't t know their source,
from the ether or my mind?
I need to find calm, of course.

Like the snail moving slow,
taking life in his slide,
he just moves along and if a threat does come,
in his shell, he pops to hide.

Snails seem leisurely, as they go,
where they are going, I dont know,
thinking of a snails movement,
my heart to beat more slow.

I tell myself , just keep going like a snail,
no matter how long the journey takes,
enjoy the scenery, calm my heart,
and dont worry about mistakes.

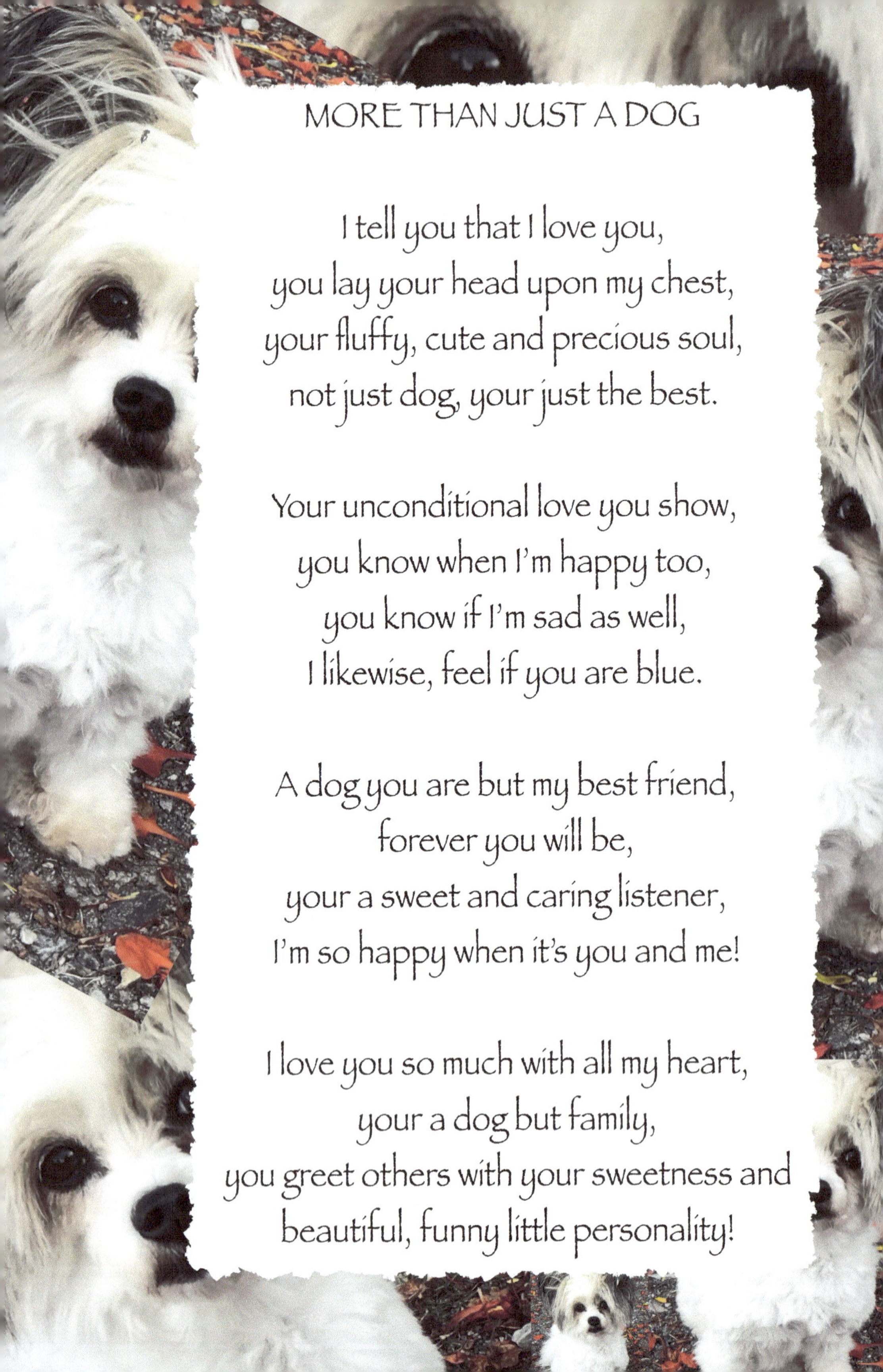

MORE THAN JUST A DOG

I tell you that I love you,
you lay your head upon my chest,
your fluffy, cute and precious soul,
not just dog, your just the best.

Your unconditional love you show,
you know when I'm happy too,
you know if I'm sad as well,
I likewise, feel if you are blue.

A dog you are but my best friend,
forever you will be,
your a sweet and caring listener,
I'm so happy when it's you and me!

I love you so much with all my heart,
your a dog but family,
you greet others with your sweetness and
beautiful, funny little personality!

SHADOW GLOW

From the darkness,
shines some light,
a glow from far away,
it warms thy eyes and lifts me up,
a dawn of a new day.

Shadows form where there is no bright,
without bright, they cant exist,
the edges where, light meets dark,
I think you get the gist.

A shadow doesn't glow at all,
its the glow that gives it shape,
the light shining from the other side,
another world, structure or landscape.

Shadows metaphorical,
the pain, the guilt the shame,
all the lower vibrational states,
face them dont disclaim.

To deny ones shadows keeps them dark,
only to peep in times of sad,
amplified when light is scarce,
love light, takes away the bad.

Love, thankfulness and gratitude,
shines light beams from within,
shadows they grow smaller then,
and inside your glow therein.

Shadow glow, smile and woe,
both have their place in life,
vibrate higher, giving thanks,
self love keeps you out of strife.

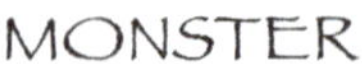

MONSTER

There's a monster in us all,
the one we try to hide,
every now and then and sometimes,
we show our monster side.

Yes we all are human,
it's the emotional side I mean,
we can be kind and playful,
monster nowhere to be seen,

But if the monster wants some air,
he awaits the problem to come,
and then he jumps ....out to play,
hot and angry like the sun!

Its ok, monster has a right to live,
he only wants to roar,
he gets tired of being all cooped up,
It's no wonder that he swore.

The monster in us all,
in the end isn't always bad,
he just wants to come out and breathe a bit,
to help take away our mad.

There's a monster in us all,
the one we try to hide,
sometimes though he must come out,
to balance your life in stride.

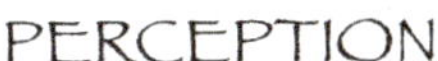

PERCEPTION

Perception is a point of view,
we all have many of those,
sometimes with others we think in sync,
and to some, difference means your foes.

Angles, angles, minds that think, eyes that see,
so many different ideas everywhere,
some are fortunate to see colours,
and there are those that cannot, not fair.

We all have our own individual stance,
on views, beliefs and the like.
just because opinions are not like yours,
please dont tell people to get on their bike.

Now there are things like ethics and morality,
of course these things are of importance,
for uniting us all, even with different opinions,
so we can smile together at a glance.

Perceptions will, always be varied,
from me to you and them,
just accepting this and moving forward,
please be kind to your fellow human.

Now you see this entire poem,
is my perceptions too, you see,
just sharing a thought or two, with you,
my mind, my heart and me.

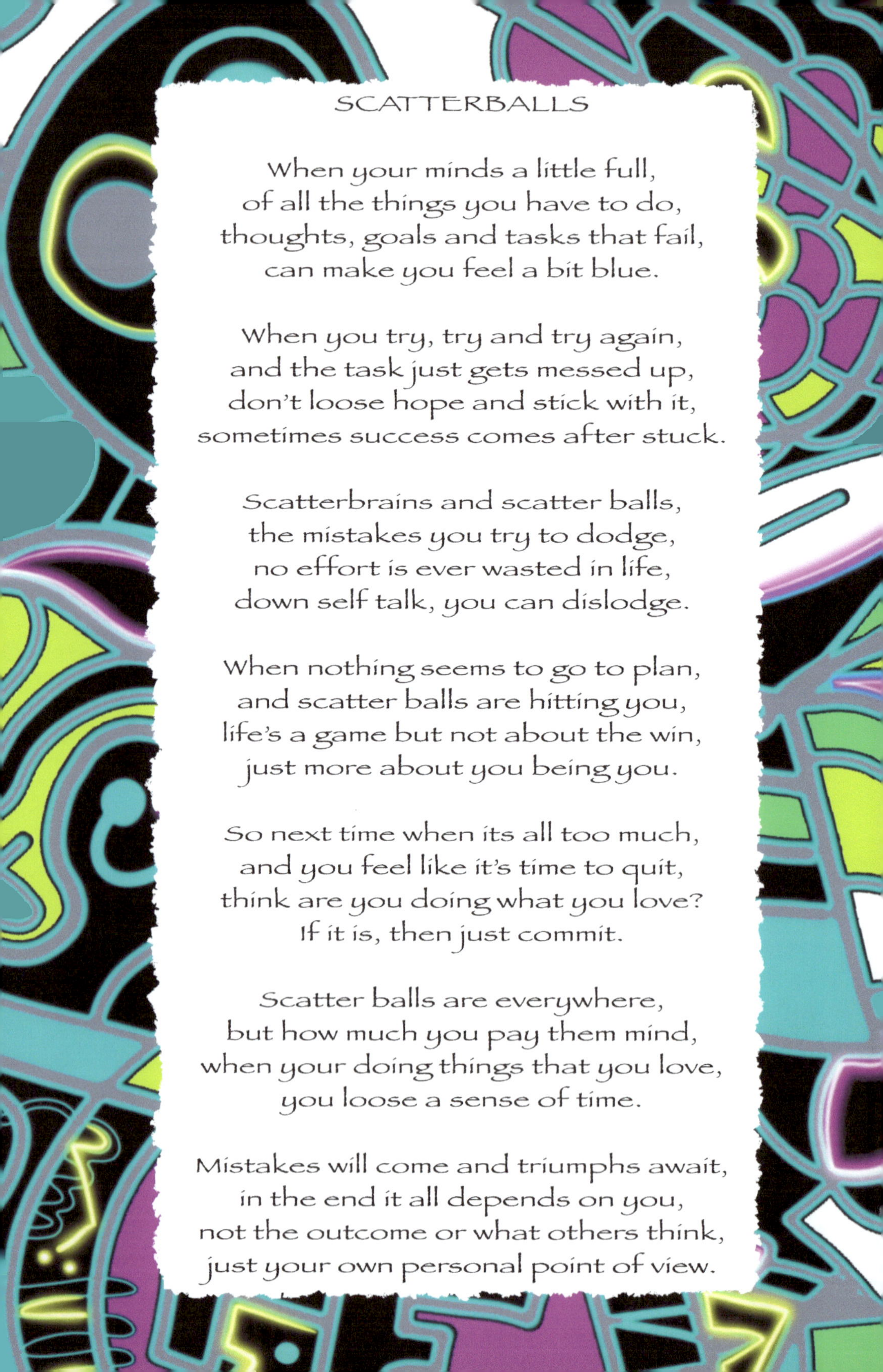

SCATTERBALLS

When your minds a little full,
of all the things you have to do,
thoughts, goals and tasks that fail,
can make you feel a bit blue.

When you try, try and try again,
and the task just gets messed up,
don't loose hope and stick with it,
sometimes success comes after stuck.

Scatterbrains and scatter balls,
the mistakes you try to dodge,
no effort is ever wasted in life,
down self talk, you can dislodge.

When nothing seems to go to plan,
and scatter balls are hitting you,
life's a game but not about the win,
just more about you being you.

So next time when its all too much,
and you feel like it's time to quit,
think are you doing what you love?
If it is, then just commit.

Scatter balls are everywhere,
but how much you pay them mind,
when your doing things that you love,
you loose a sense of time.

Mistakes will come and triumphs await,
in the end it all depends on you,
not the outcome or what others think,
just your own personal point of view.

UNIQUE

I feel like I am different,
weird and not like the rest,
I believe in multiverses,
and that life is a just a test.

Quantum physics tells us,
that nothing is as it seems,
matter is not solid,
molecules vibrating at frequencies.

The universe is vast,
enormous in its size,
or is that just our perception,
and were all living in our minds?

Theres a theory of holographic,
the space that we live in,
maybe we are just avatars,
In a game we're trying to win.

Universes of parallel,
crops circles, aliens and magic,
dimensions, space, the plank scale,
all the things that defy logic.

these are just some interests,
I have such an open mind,
sometimes I feel like I'm from out of space,
and not like human kind.

I feel like I am different,
maybe you do too?
I'd love to find beings more like me,
and discover things with you!

Heres to all the unique dreamers,
eccentrics and weirdos,
just be you dont conform,
and be your own hero!

OBSTICORNER

Plodding along you know,
and things are going swell,
smiles are big and life is good,
then along comes a bombshell.

Hurdles to jump and obstacles present,
now smiles turn upside down,
new corners to take, unprepared,
all of a sudden I'm wearing a frown!

Ok now, now, let's, reassess,
the situation in front at hand,
take a breath reevaluate,
it's just something that was not planned.

A moment of pause I must give me,
to think about a new approach,
maybe I need to learn some more,
research or find a coach.

One thing is, I know for sure,
that I will not give up,
just turn these corners as best I can,
then go and fill my cup.

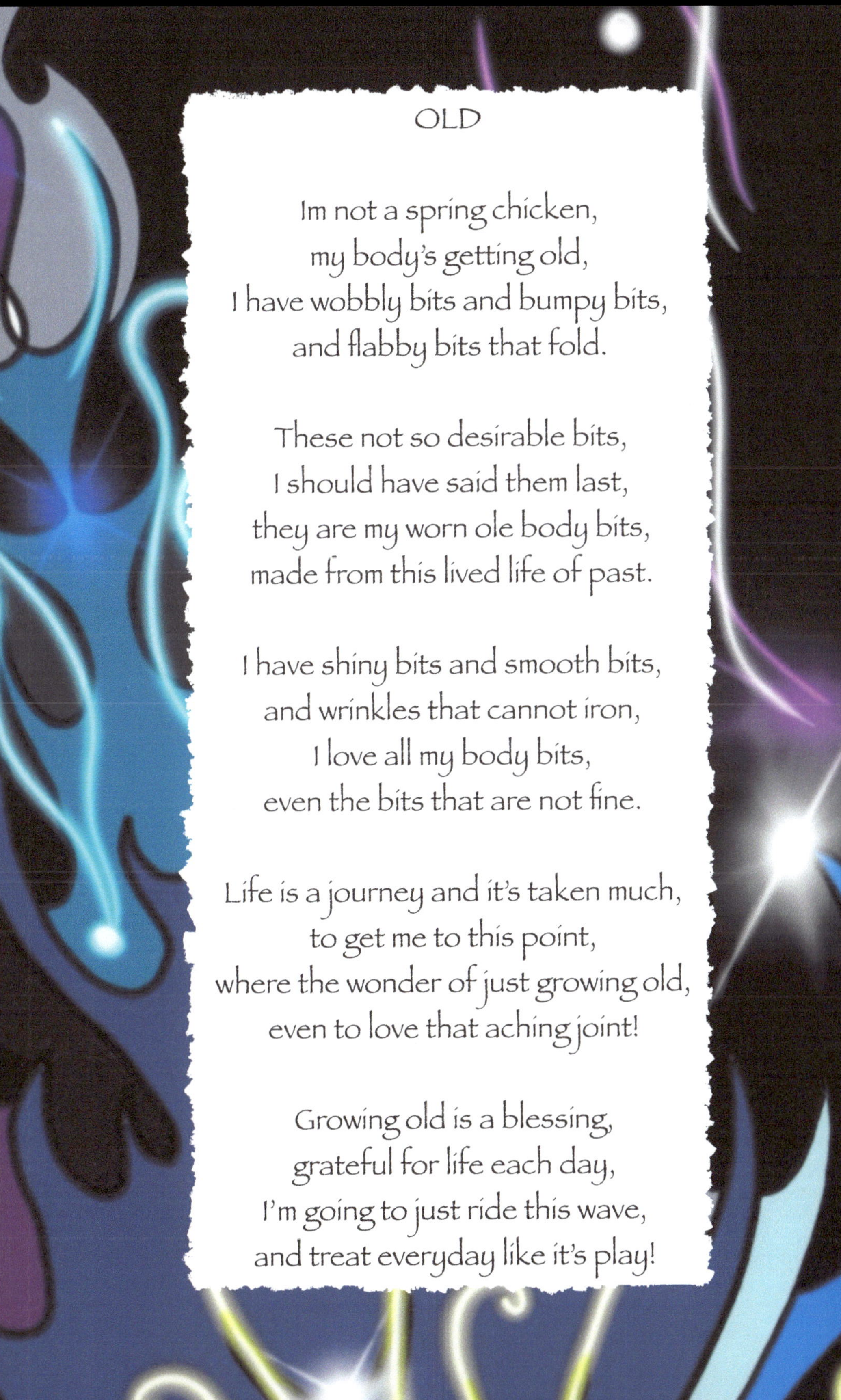

OLD

Im not a spring chicken,
my body's getting old,
I have wobbly bits and bumpy bits,
and flabby bits that fold.

These not so desirable bits,
I should have said them last,
they are my worn ole body bits,
made from this lived life of past.

I have shiny bits and smooth bits,
and wrinkles that cannot iron,
I love all my body bits,
even the bits that are not fine.

Life is a journey and it's taken much,
to get me to this point,
where the wonder of just growing old,
even to love that aching joint!

Growing old is a blessing,
grateful for life each day,
I'm going to just ride this wave,
and treat everyday like it's play!

BUBBLES

Bubbles, bubbles, bubbles,
are there bubbles in outer space?
bubbles, bubbles, bubbles,
can be found all over the place.

Bubbles in the bath
and bubbles in your drink,
bubbles in the washing machine,
and bubbles in the sink.

Bubbles are nice and round,
and can float throughout the air,
these bubbles are being blown about,
by lots of things everywhere!

Bubbles can be soapy,
bubbles inside you make you burp,
sometimes bubbles get inside you,
when you swallow air and slurp.

Bubbles, bubbles, bubbles,
so sparkly in the sun,
bubbles, bubbles, bubbles,
blowing them is so fun!

Bubbles, bubbles, bubbles,
don't last for long sometime,
they pop and burst and disappear,
the higher that they climb.

Bubbles, bubbles, bubbles,
are in plastic wrap for post,
helping breakables not to break,
for bumpy trips up the coast.

Bubbles, bubbles, bubbles,
it's time to end this here,
just like a bubble,
it's time to disappear.

BLUE

Today I'm feeling kinda blue.
sad and down and guilty too.

Someone I love got angry at me,
I yelled back reciprocating energy.

I can't go back in time and undo,
I said I'm sorry for the things I did to you.

I've grown a lot and changed my ways,
happiness I've found now in my days.

My advice is just trying to help you through,
make amends to those in my life and you.

The past is gone we cannot go back,
so please let's grow,
say gratitudes not lack.

Life is a dance and not a straight line,
can't think of all the bad stuff,
otherwise it'll just have you cryin.

Today I'm feeling like the dark clouds cover me,
I just wish those I love could live happily.

People change, yes traumas are real.
face, then release them away,
then see how better you feel.

Today I'm feeling kinda blue,
I know it will just pass,
I love you and I love me too,
for love will always last.

THE GAP

The gap between us gets bigger,
as we age in seperate ways,
the distance between our viewpoints,
seems to be changing with the days.

We used to be much closer,
the fun we used to share,
but growth has a funny way of changing us,
sometimes the change is hard to bear.

I feel the change within me,
I am not the person I used to be,
I see you repeating same old patterns,
.... and it really saddens me.

But who am I to judge you?
for your life is all your own,
I just want to share with you the things I've learnt,
asking you to rethink all that you've known.

Everyone grows at different rates,
and some never grow at all.
helping others with their problems is rewarding,
and so, so sad to see them fall.

What to do is the conundrum,
to help but not control,
for the when the advice that is given,
comes peacefully from heart and soul.

I wish that we could grow together,
however, the reality is not so,
I just really hope the love we have,
Is stronger than us turning foe.

The gap between us seems so large,
I want to make it small,
the fix I think, is by talking lots,
not hiding behind a wall.

I love you, you are dear to me,
I just want you to be alright,
nowing that you're healthy and well,
so we can both sleep peacefully at night.

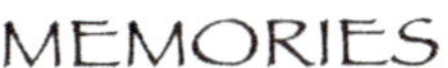

MEMORIES

Memories of sadness,
memories of fun,
memories of madness,
memories of hum.

Lingering memories repeat on a loop,
ponders of many kind,
thinking, thinking, thinking ,
...will have loose your mind.

Stop pause, be boss of your brain,
don't follow thoughts of every life strain.

Memories of heartache,
memories of smiles,
memories of who you used to be,
memories of old times.

Memories are past times,
things that have occurred,
switching to the future thoughts,
and some dreams feel absurd.

Tomorrow comes and gone is yesterday.
memories are just memories,
look around and see today!

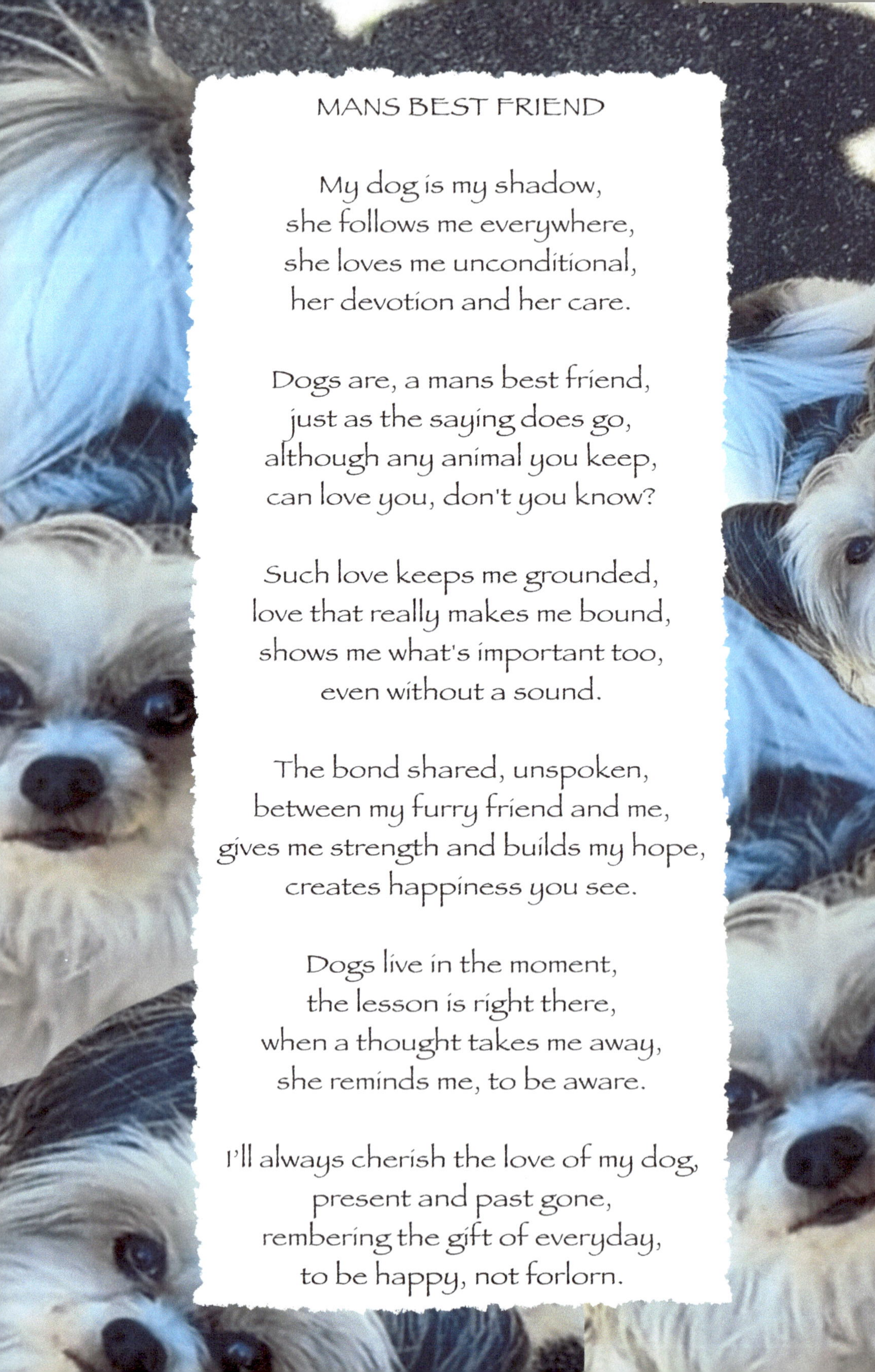

MANS BEST FRIEND

My dog is my shadow,
she follows me everywhere,
she loves me unconditional,
her devotion and her care.

Dogs are, a mans best friend,
just as the saying does go,
although any animal you keep,
can love you, don't you know?

Such love keeps me grounded,
love that really makes me bound,
shows me what's important too,
even without a sound.

The bond shared, unspoken,
between my furry friend and me,
gives me strength and builds my hope,
creates happiness you see.

Dogs live in the moment,
the lesson is right there,
when a thought takes me away,
she reminds me, to be aware.

I'll always cherish the love of my dog,
present and past gone,
rembering the gift of everyday,
to be happy, not forlorn.

BIG TECH

As technology increases
phones, tablets and the like,
towers, signals and wavelengths,
how much of it you like?

My body cannot choose,
which energy goes inside,
the power turned on so much,
and frequency so high!

We all emit an energy,
as do the trees, oceans and waves,
animals and all living things,
and of course, the suns hot blaze.

Our precious earth is filling up,
with all this man made junk,
sometimes I wish I could grab it all,
and take it to the dump.

The sky is full of satellites,
and space is not immune,
now the man wants to go way up,
and put more junk on the moon!

I crave a time of simpler things,
when nature had more trees,
you had to grow your own food,
and meadows had more bees.

I wish I could change technology,
to find a better way,
it makes me sad to contemplate,
the world as it is today.

As technology increases,
and man looks into his phone,
I feel that the connection,
is not with earth our home.

SMALL STEPS

One foot in front of the other,
step by step is how you move,
changing your position,
to find your groovy, groove.

Metaphorically im speaking,
just do each day what you can,
towards something that you seek.
just get started make a plan.

You can move your thoughts,
visualise your dreams,
train your mind you see,
keep those visions,
dont give up......
be all that you can be.

Small steps, one little step each day,
is all that it can take,
go on you, get moving,
and see what you can make.

Now I'm not being bossy,
it's you I want to inspire,
to take the action in your own life,
and be the you, you will admire!!

WITHIN

When I turn my eyes around,
and have a look within,
I notice if it's a frown I wear,
or a big fat grin.

My body is on auto-pilot,
doing as it may like,
when I notice my body,
I feel all the bits, that are quite tight.

My body is my temple,
sometimes I treat it bad,
my cells respond to feelings,
yes, even when I'm mad.

My body is made of water,
my emotions set the tone,
for ripples to be sent throughout,
right down to the very bone.

Emotions have a frequency,
how subtle that maybe,
when we choose to tune in,
we see what makes us be.

Our mind and body are linked,
in so many ways can you see?
everything is bundled together,
we are the same, yes you and me.

Body and conciousness,
are so delicately entwined,
the body responds in every cell,
to what's happening in your mind.

My goal in life is to notice,
and honour the world within,
rectify the broken bits
and find like minded kin.

I believe we all want the same things,
on deep level within our heart,
love, happiness a life of meaning,
to the end, and from the start.

THE HEART

The heart doesnt get to choose,
the emotions that it can feel,
they come and go with influence,
some imagined and some real.

The heart can lead us astray,
or bring you to your knees,
it can make you fall in love,
and play the birds and bees.

The heart can be so fickle,
and have you all confused,
leaving you all muddled up,
or laughing and amused.

The heart is linked with the brain,
and its hard to choose a leader,
sometimes the question is so hard,
so much you cant choose either.

The heart knows more, than what we think,
it's the circumstance you see,
the heart cant always have its way,
the mind says its not easy.

The heart feels, with each beat,
oh the brain, think, think, think...
one is filled with emotions,
and the other with logic.

So many times they are not in-sync,
the answer is not always clear,
the heart wants, what the heart wants,
and the brain is full of fear.

So in the end its hard to choose,
so frustrating tut, tut, tut......
I think its best to forget them both...
and just listen to the gut!

RANDOM

Random flow, twisty lines,
shapes and curvy turns,
bright and cheerful colours,
art takes away concerns.

What can you see here?
in this little abstract?
nothing is definitive,
in abstract, that's a fact!

I see a butterfly, a bird or even mole?
how about a running man?
I went down a rabbit hole!

Beady, dots and leaf like things,
and blobby little bits,
rainbow tones and ziggy zags,
and light codes in the mix!

Art is fun, creative brain,
it's fun when your in there,
you know, the right side of your brain,
underneath your hair.

Hope this little draw today,
makes you think a bit,
or rather that you just have fun,
deep breathe and look and sit.

Now to conclude this little rhyme,
I wish you a lovely day,
have a stretch, unclench your jaw,
sending love and light your way.

KEEP ON

Keep on keeping on,
hey you, never give up,
your future is exciting,
look, half full is your cup.

Your life is all your making,
strive on and then, get some rest,
each day, move towards your dream,
and know you did your best.

Dont listen to the haters,
the ones who pull you down,
your smile is your power,
happiness is not found in your frown.

Hormones and emotions,
are inadvertedly linked,
sometimes they can take a hold,
change them moods before you've blinked.

Oxytocin, gaba, testosterone,
and dopamines,
oestrogen, serotonin,
and fun filled endorphins.

Knowledge is awareness,
of moods your body is in,
learning it's just the body doing stuff,
don't stress and you will win.

Everything will change,
even hormones have to adjust,
control your body with your mind,
and deep breathing is a must.

This is my little poem,
of my self talk.....I do to me,
sharing with you what I've learnt,
on my road to be happy.

2021

Where has my happy gone?
in a world that has gone mad,
it's taking all my strength to smile,
watching people loose all they had.

The government is lying,
TV and corporations rule,
I just cant watch all this madness,
it's making people so cruel.

My smile comes out and then it fades,
by the energies I feel,
so much sadness, and loss of hope,
what's happening, seems unreal.

My heart's been broken,
the government is to blame,
pushing humans all around,
like pieces in their game.

The world has forever changed,
there's no going back,
we have to make a new,
make new friends and family,
to replace the ones that flew.

We cannot make any others see,
of a world that they choose not,
we have to hold dear in heart,
the ones of us who've not forgot.

There's more at play in this world of ours,
the answers are deep within,
finding our soul connections,
higher self and like minded kin.

I don't have all the answers,
but I know one thing is true,
I will always believe in following my gut,
to help me feel less blue.

Today I felt a small creative spark,
which led me to write this verse,
I felt a voice inside me whisper,
you're not alone in this universe.

I want to share this poem,
my heart just had to say,
if your hurting too, dear human,
I send you a hug today.

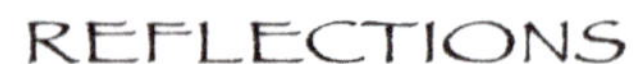

REFLECTIONS

Reflections in a mirror,
reflections in your mind,
both conjure up emotions,
good and bad that you will find.

Refections of many kinds,
we think about in life,
the peace, calm and stillness of 'NOW',
only some thoughts deserve a slice.

Hindsight and foresight,
look in front of you,
just focus on the task at hand,
to create a thing of new.

Life is a journey,
days, months and years,
reflecting memories linger in mind,
repeating all your fears.

Reflecting can be happy,
please don't get me wrong,
but if all your times spent reflecting,
your life's progress will prelong.

Reflections in a mirror,
say "I love you" to your reflecting me,
utilise this life, you have right now,
and be as amazing as you can be!

PORTAL

Portal from another world,
a doorway to another realm,
do you decide to peek inside?
your choice you take the helm.

Port hole window on a ship,
a familiar opening,
for we know what's on the other side,
water, fish, waves that sort of thing.

Reality questions on what we see,
is life bona fide or a dream?
does reality exist only if it's tangible?
believing in the unseen extreme?

Portal in and portal out?
I imagine them like a black hole,
I also imagine them imaginary,
some would say I've lost control.

I think that our ... minds 3rd eye,
when open, can show so much,
it shows us things not all can see,
feel, smell or even touch!

Portal, portal hey you mortal,
is this really just THE matrix?
life is all just a simulation?
higher self test, psychometrics?

Weird, deep, far out man!
my mind open to all ideas you know,
is this world round or flat?
are we living like a 'TRUMAN' show?

Never ending knowledge,
the search will never end,
I'm going to question everything,
on my journey of life, till I transcend.

THIS MOMENT

Birds chirp in the distance,
the washing machine makes a hum,
the wind blows softly through the curtain door,
what has my life become?

Questions of the future,
questions from the past,
none of them quite matter,
breathe, heart beat slow, not fast.

Mind empty moment,
just listening to the ambience,
feel inward, close my eyes and
feel the going of the tense.

Lots of sounds all around,
the trick is to quiet my mind,
just sitting in the now,
and harmony I will find.

Right now I surrender,
to all that I cannot control,
I want to flow like water,
and be at peace as I grow old.

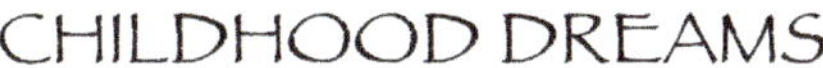

CHILDHOOD DREAMS

Just for a moment, close your eyes,
try, remember yourself at 5 or 8,
can you think of all your dreams back then,
and all the things that you could make?

Childhood dreams and wonder,
seem to fade alot as we grow,
but they are not really, forever gone,
they can come back yes, don't you know?

Just for a moment close your eyes,
listen to the whispers of your mind,
feel the magic and excitment,
and the desires you had, you will find.

Life gets in the way sometimes,
of the goals that we once had,
you can always truly find them again,
to where your heart feels glad.

Just for a moment close your eyes,
yes you grownup, hey, please listen you!
You can create your dreams you know,
just take steps to make them come true!

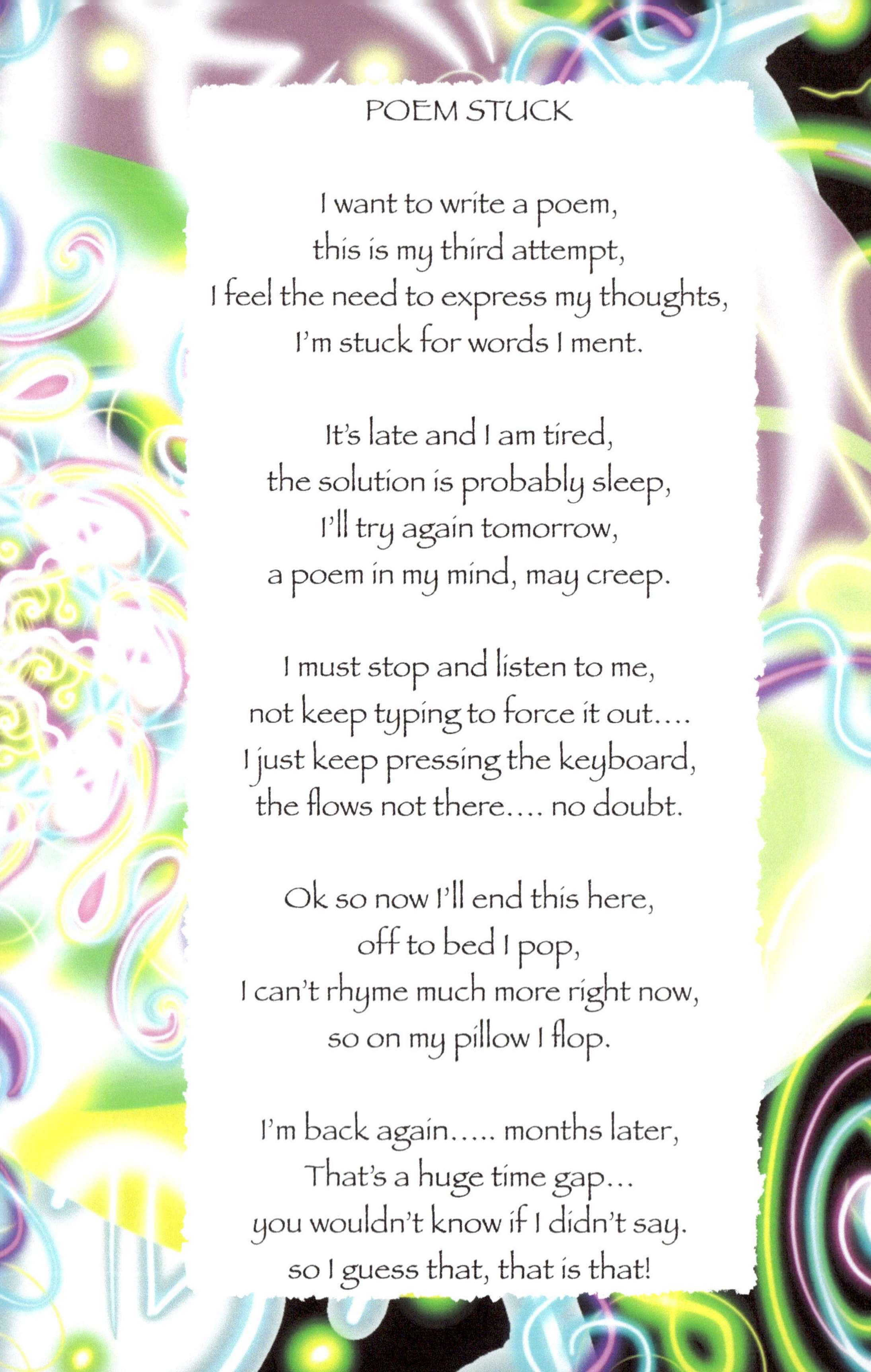

POEM STUCK

I want to write a poem,
this is my third attempt,
I feel the need to express my thoughts,
I'm stuck for words I ment.

It's late and I am tired,
the solution is probably sleep,
I'll try again tomorrow,
a poem in my mind, may creep.

I must stop and listen to me,
not keep typing to force it out....
I just keep pressing the keyboard,
the flows not there.... no doubt.

Ok so now I'll end this here,
off to bed I pop,
I can't rhyme much more right now,
so on my pillow I flop.

I'm back again..... months later,
That's a huge time gap...
you wouldn't know if I didn't say.
so I guess that, that is that!

BABY GIRLS

My two baby girls,
you're all older and have grown,
you've flown the nest,
now you've made your home.

We've sure have had our ups,
and we've sure had our downs,
our bonds have been tested,
through the heartaches and the frowns.

Through the pain and the tears though,
we have had lots of fun,
from the moment you both were born,
my loves never been undone.

Through the the thick and thin,
I just want you to know,
I will always treasure the times
and watching you both grow.

Just so you know that,
for forever you will be,
both in my heart together,
you're such a big part of me.

At the end of the day,
remember love is what is true,
I hope you are both happy,
in what ever that you do.

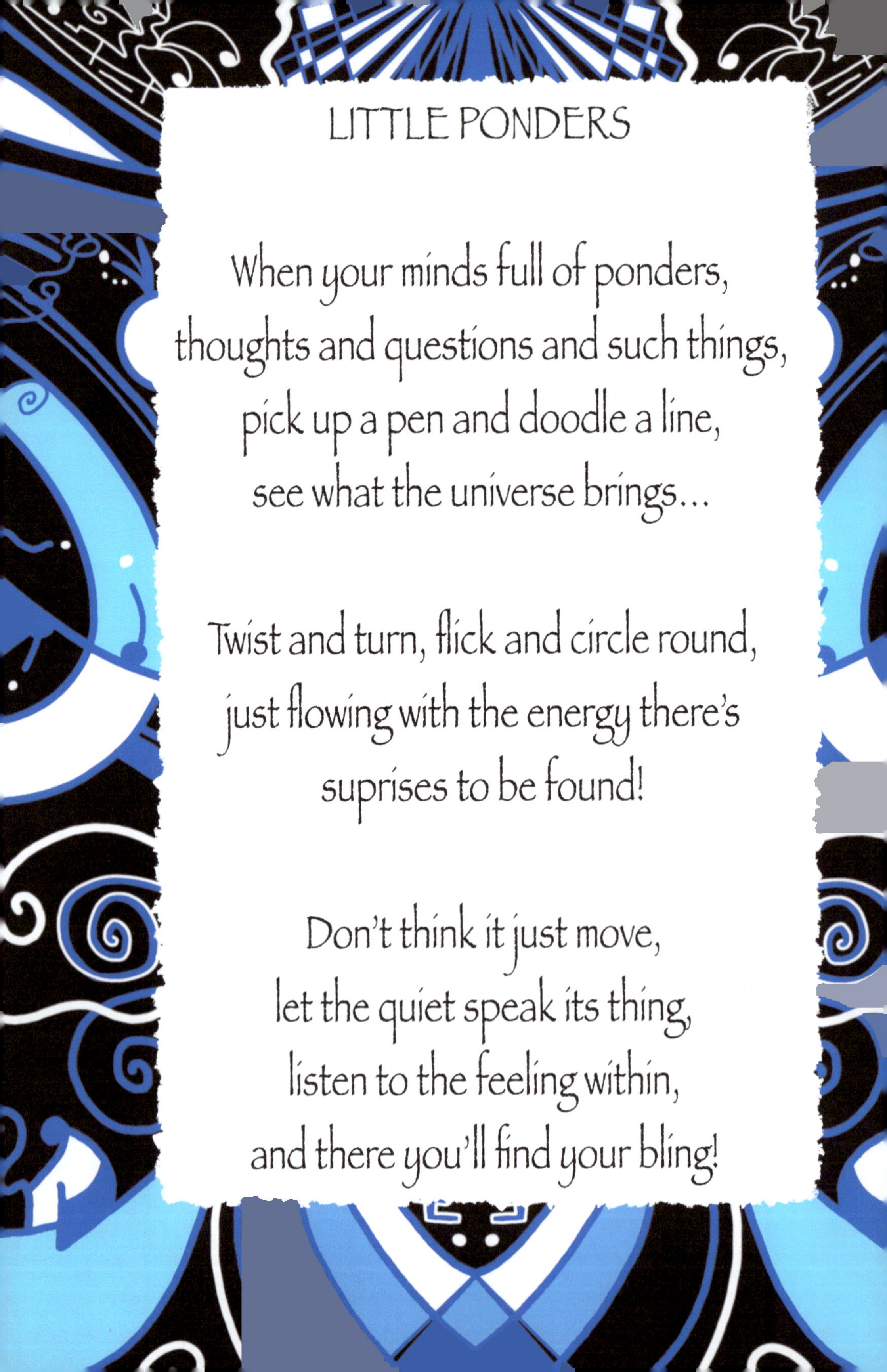

LITTLE PONDERS

When your minds full of ponders,
thoughts and questions and such things,
pick up a pen and doodle a line,
see what the universe brings...

Twist and turn, flick and circle round,
just flowing with the energy there's
suprises to be found!

Don't think it just move,
let the quiet speak its thing,
listen to the feeling within,
and there you'll find your bling!

RHYTHM

I have a certain rhythm,
in the poems that I write,
I like to make the words rhyme,
try and try as I might.

I love honest poetry,
words coming from the soul,
sharing the emotion,
and a story to be told.

I think poems are like music,
it's in our DNA,
just like tunes that make you bounce,
evoke, feelings make you sway.

Words are so powerful,
I mean it when they're said,
careful of what you utter,
for they linger.. in ones head.

Poetry is an expression,
of what your feeling on the inside,
bringing forward and sharing,
so others can read and find.

I like my poems to move,
pull a heartstring or two,
or bring a moment of happy,
a bit of joy for you.

Life is wonderful and fleeting,
enjoy it while you are here,
create your dreams, live, be free,
there's magic, dont you fear.

I have a certain rhythm,
in the poems that I write,
I hope this poem makes you smile,
and brings you love and light.

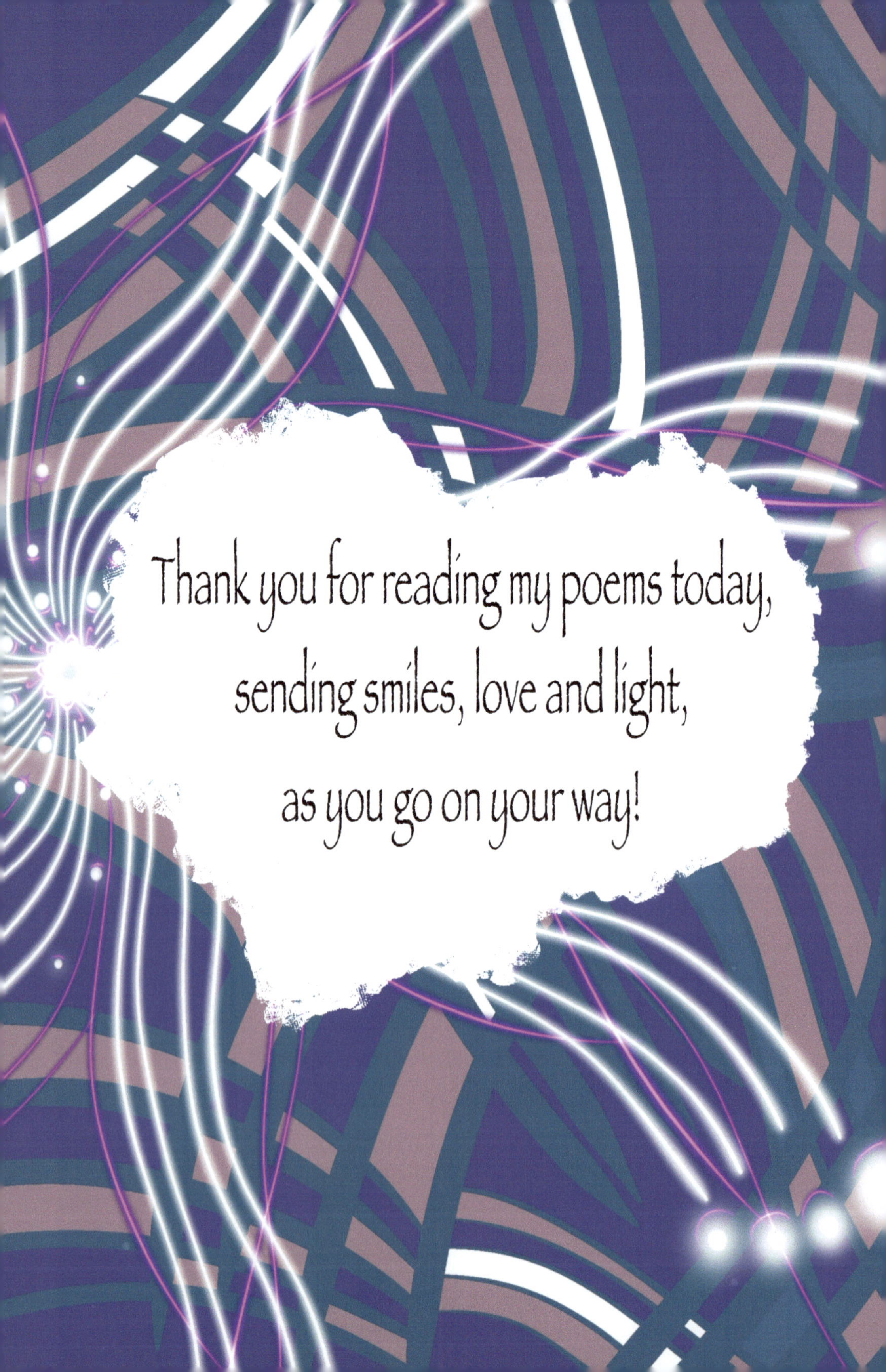
Thank you for reading my poems today,
sending smiles, love and light,
as you go on your way!